Look and Find®

Disney

THE
LION KING

Illustrated by
Jaime Diaz Studios

Cover illustrated by
Don Williams and H.R. Russell

Published by
Louis Weber, C.E.O.
Publications International, Ltd.
7373 North Cicero Avenue
Lincolnwood, Illinois 60712

Ground Floor, 59 Gloucester Place
London, W1U 8JJ

Customer Service: customer_service@pilbooks.com

www.pilbooks.com

p i kids is a trademark of Publications International, Ltd.,
and is registered in the United States.
Look and Find is a trademark of Publications International, Ltd.,
and is registered in the United States and Canada.

8 7 6 5 4 3 2 1

Manufactured in China.

ISBN: 978-1-4508-5631-7

publications international, ltd.

A new morning brings a cub to Mufasa and Sarabi. The animals of the Pride Lands have gathered to watch Simba take the first steps of his life's journey.

Simba begins the search for his place in the Circle of Life as Rafiki presents him to the kingdom. Along with Simba and Rafiki, see if you can find the others who have gathered for this wonderful celebration.

Mufasa and Sarabi

Zazu

Nala

Scar

Shenzi, Banzai, and Ed

Simba can't wait until he is king. Then no one will tell *him* what to do or where to go. He begins to imagine just what it will be like to finally be in charge.

Simba's imagination runs away with him. Can you find these royal objects in Simba's fantasy kingdom?

Simba

His Queen

His advisor

His crown

His herald

His scout

His portrait

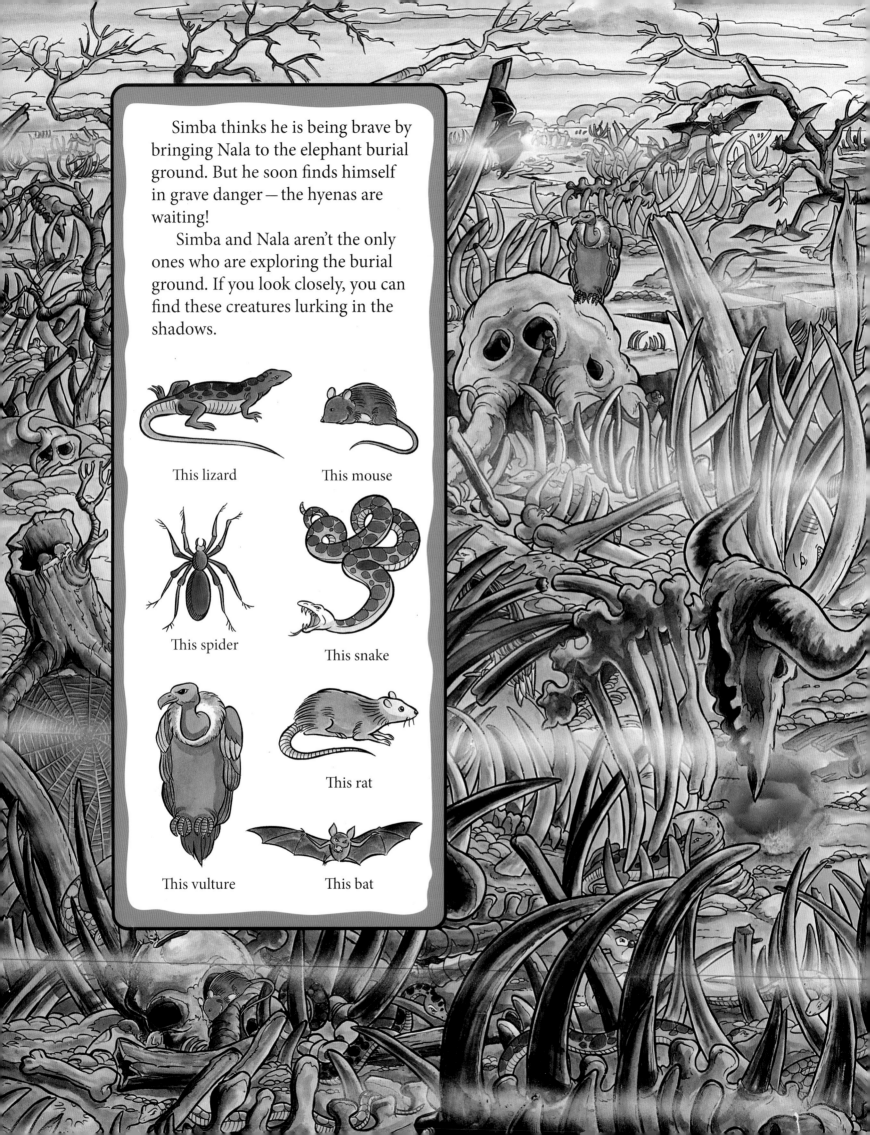

Simba thinks he is being brave by bringing Nala to the elephant burial ground. But he soon finds himself in grave danger — the hyenas are waiting!

Simba and Nala aren't the only ones who are exploring the burial ground. If you look closely, you can find these creatures lurking in the shadows.

This lizard

This mouse

This spider

This snake

This vulture

This rat

This bat

Hakuna Matata! A wonderful phrase, indeed! Simba finds two new friends in Pumbaa the warthog and Timon the meerkat. They help the young cub forget his worries.

Can you find these worry-free and fun-loving animals as they frolic in the jungle?

Simba

Pumbaa

Timon

This hedgehog

This mongoose

This turtle

This bird

This anteater

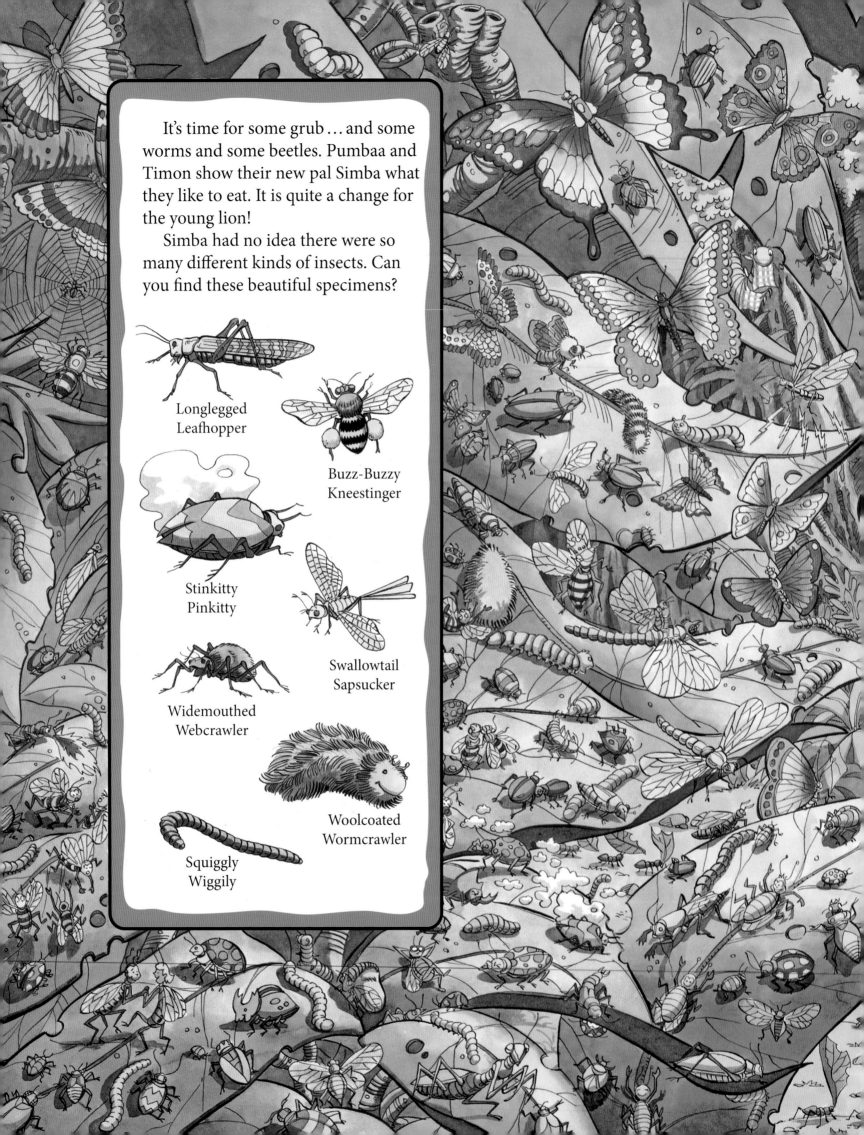

It's time for some grub … and some worms and some beetles. Pumbaa and Timon show their new pal Simba what they like to eat. It is quite a change for the young lion!

Simba had no idea there were so many different kinds of insects. Can you find these beautiful specimens?

Longlegged Leafhopper

Buzz-Buzzy Kneestinger

Stinkitty Pinkitty

Swallowtail Sapsucker

Widemouthed Webcrawler

Woolcoated Wormcrawler

Squiggly Wiggily

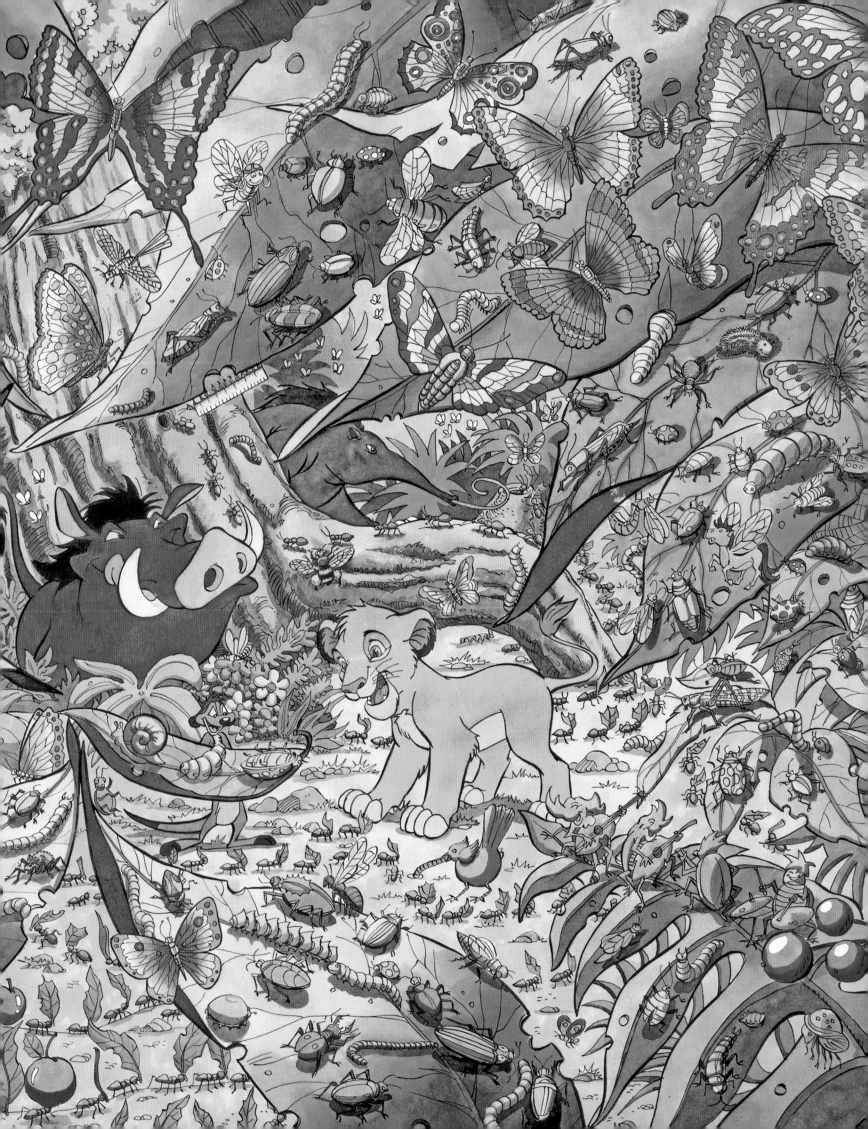

Maybe it's the moonlight, but Simba and Nala find themselves in a romantic mood now that they're together again. As they look around, everything seems to be in the shape of a heart. Can you find these hearts?

These storks

This tree

This bug

This rock

This flower

This butterfly

This bird

These vines

It is a dark, sad day at Pride Rock. Scar has taken over and has allowed the hyenas to wreak havoc. Now the savannah is nothing more than a wasteland.

Except for the hyenas, Scar has caused almost all the animals to leave. Look closely to find a few who remain.

Sarabi

Scar

Banzai

The scout

Zazu

Shenzi

Ed

A vulture

Simba realises it is time to stop running from the past. He returns to Pride Rock to challenge Scar for his place as king.

With a mighty roar, Simba battles his terrified uncle while his friends take on the hyenas. Can you find these frightening hyenas?

The Circle of Life is complete. Simba and Nala are now the proud parents of their own cub. Like his father before him, the newborn cub is presented to the kingdom by wise Rafiki.

Simba and Nala aren't the only proud parents in the Pride Lands. See if you can find these newborns.

This zebra foal

This elephant calf

This giraffe calf

This gazelle calf

This ostrich chick

This cheetah cub

This hippo calf

This rhino calf

Creatures from far and wide came to see the ceremony of Simba's birth. Can you spot these animals whose home isn't in Africa?

☐ A kangaroo
☐ A raccoon
☐ A panda
☐ An owl
☐ A skunk
☐ A fox
☐ A penguin

When Simba is pretending he is king, his imagination runs wild. Can you spot these wacky animals he has envisioned?

☐ A yellow zebra
☐ An orange hippo
☐ A green giraffe
☐ A purple elephant
☐ A polka-dotted antelope
☐ A pink rhino
☐ A blue ostrich

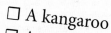

Go back to the burial ground to find more hidden animals.

☐ A Saint Bernard
☐ A kangaroo
☐ A penguin
☐ A koala
☐ An eagle
☐ A shark

"Hakuna Matata!" Go back to the jungle to find these playful monkeys.

☐ A splashing monkey
☐ A constructive monkey
☐ A lazy monkey
☐ A monkey-see-and-doer
☐ An itchy monkey
☐ A juggling monkey
☐ A curious monkey
☐ A thirsty monkey

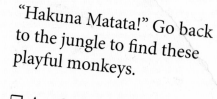